Seawater

Women's Voices from the Shores of the Caribbean Leeward Islands

**Anguilla
Nevis
St. Kitts**

Doreen Crick

Cover and Storytelling Art by Esme Archer-Rousell

Seawater
Copyright © 2018 by Doreen Crick

All rights reserved. No part of this publication may be reproduced, distributed, or transmitted in any form or by any means, including photocopying, recording, or other electronic or mechanical methods, without the prior written permission of the author, except in the case of brief quotations embodied in critical reviews and certain other non-commercial uses permitted by copyright law.

Tellwell Talent
www.tellwell.ca

ISBN
978-0-2288-0499-4 (Hardcover)
978-0-2288-0497-0 (Paperback)
978-0-2288-0500-7 (eBook)

Table of Contents

Foreword vii
Prologue ix
My Story xiii
Introduction xv

Chapter 1   Our route to the Caribbean................................ 1
Chapter 2   Immigrants to the Leeward Islands 10
Chapter 3   Introductions to the three islands – Anguilla, Nevis
            and St. Christopher (later referred to as St. Kitts)............16
Chapter 4   The Island of Nevis...21
Chapter 5   The Island of St. Christopher – "St. Kitts".......24
Chapter 6   The Promise of Freedom 35
Chapter 7   The experience of slaves along the Eastern
            Seaboard of North America 40
Chapter 8   READ ALL ABOUT IT: BLACKSTRAP MOLASSES…..........45

Epilogue: Voices from the shores of the Caribbean...........................47

I dedicate this book,
Seawater, to my husband, Reginald Crick.

Foreword

It gives me great pleasure to write the foreword for Doreen Crick's book. I have known her as a great friend for many years and I find her vibrant personality and enthusiasm for life infectious. She is very engaged in everyday current affairs and loves to discuss topics relating to history, education, health, culture and our youth. She proudly admits to being eighty-five years 'young' and believes strongly that, "it is not the number of years in your life, but the amount of life in your years," that really matters. I asked Doreen the question, "Why do you want to write this book?" She replied:

"At this stage in my life I have to be intentional in the topics I choose to pursue and I choose this book as my priority."

Doreen learned great lessons from the stories told by her grandmother and other women whose ancestors grew up in the Caribbean Islands of St Kitts, Nevis and Anguilla in the early nineteenth century (the 1800s). Their stories demonstrate how British Colonialism and slavery directly impacted the lives of people on the islands and left indelible marks on the generations. Some of the images, created by the stories Doreen shares in her book, transport us back to a time and place when people were enslaved and brought to these beautiful tropical islands for enforced labour to enrich the coffers of the British Crown. In spite of the hardships endured, the women shone through in heroic ways by working hard to protect their families and making decisions which would ultimately ensure better lives for their children and generations to come.

SEAWATER, the title of her Doreen's book, symbolizes many things. The islands are surrounded by *seawater* on all sides; it also symbolizes the oceans on which the ships sailed to bring their priceless human cargo to this region of the world. In addition *seawater* provided a source of a precious commodity, sodium chloride otherwise known as salt. It is a valuable preservative of meats and other foods necessary for survival in the absence of refrigeration and it has been a valuable source of income for the inhabitants of this area.

In this book, Doreen is creating an historical legacy in her attempt to translate the Colonial history of her Caribbean people into a simple format to educate, inspire and enlighten teenagers, especially her own grandchildren. She emphasises the power of the survival instinct of these Island women, their bravery in the face of great oppression and determination to use circumstances to their advantage to overcome adversity.

Doreen believes proper education is the key to bridging the gap between our Colonial past and the present generation. She hopes to add a voice to this discussion and in the process help to create a positive mental image in our youth as being productive, high-achieving young persons who are proud of who they are, not because of history but in spite of it.

T. Olive Phillips

President-Jamaican Cultural Assoc. of Nova Scotia, (JCANS)

June 26th 2018

Prologue

Imagine the setting: a beautiful sunset melding into a navy-blue sky speckled with glittering stars… or perhaps, the soft chorus of sea birds flying overhead, and white sandy beaches awash with playful, curling waves.

She saw him, a young lad, white—William Holman Owen—and he saw her—Eliza Fleming—black and beautiful! We great-grandchildren gave her the name of 'De-Dah'.

Their eyes met and they were hooked! Mixed marriages were not blessed by the Church at that time, however De-Dah was welcomed to live at his parent's home. They later built their own home.

Their first-born, Herbert Osborne Owen (1873 - 1944) married Marie Eglantine Barbrow. She was very beautiful, a mixture of a French and East Indian heritage. They had nine children who attended the one-room school house in Anguilla. My mother Myrtle, their first daughter, was taken out of grade three to help her mom with the children. Myrtle was smart and studied the dictionary as if it were a book of exciting literature!

Herbert spent most of his time working as the manager of the Sombrero Lighthouse. The lighthouse is located on Sombrero Island, an almost barren island 54 kilometres northwest of Antigua. It is 1.67 kilometres long by 0.38 kilometres wide, rising almost vertically from the sea to 12 meters above its surface. The lighthouse was administered by the St. Kitts, Nevis and Anguilla Government. Still today, it is the most significant pilot light for ships leaving Europe westward bound.

Anguilla, (area 37 square miles) was culturally stable—so unlike its sister islands, St. Kitts and Nevis, at that time. It is amazing!

There is so much more to tell.

'De-Dah': Great Grandmother

So much mystery about this beautiful black woman

    who was born free.

Lost in the hush-hush oblivion of

    black woman-white man

A lifetime love-bond

    but still not blessed by Mother Church.

It is time to remember her!

To reach back to the nineteenth century

    and to say, "Thanks, De-Dah,

    for being strong.

Thanks for having Great Grand-dad

Thanks for making it possible

      for my very being.

You were loved by Great Grand-dad

who stayed a lifetime by your side

Your love, together, was colour 'strong'.

Would God have thought one colour 'right'

      and another colour 'wrong'?

My Family Tree:

- 1760 Reverend Joseph Owen (second Methodist minister from England, widowed)

  - (son) David Henry Owen (1816? – 1890) married Anna Roberts (1816 – 1890)

  - (son) William Holman "Boley" Owen (1847 – 1925) and Eliza Fleming "De-Dah" Ghanaian (1857 – 1940)

  - (son) Herbert Osborne Owen (1873 – 1944) married Marie Eglantine (East Indian/English) (1874 – 1934)

  - Daughter Myrtle Blanche Owen (my mother) (1898 – 1983) married Robert Charles (Alleyne) Allen (Ghanaian//English) (1900 – 1976)

    - "Me" Blanche Doreen Allen (1933) married Reginald Ulric Crick (1932)

My Story

My Grandfather, Herbert Osborne Owen, worked at the Sombrero Lighthouse. This lighthouse is a beacon for ships sailing from Europe across the Atlantic.

We children would climb the winding spiral staircase, while counting the steps as a way to keep our attention on climbing the stairs and not looking down.

At the top we would view the horizon stretching beyond, and enjoy the scintillating splashes of sunlight on the waves. Then we would sit and watch the lighthouse keepers wash away the soot from the lens and prisms of the magnificent large lamp… for surely, 'as night will follow day,' sea captains will need that pilot light.

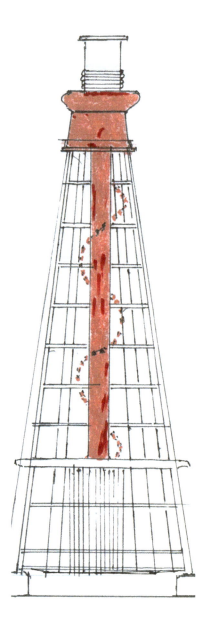

Sombrero Lighthouse

Every month a sailing ship took a supply of essentials from Anguilla to Sombrero Lighthouse.

Introduction

It has been millions of years since Pangea opened up and the wide, restless Atlantic *seawater* filled the void. It was many more years before 'human-kind' got curious about the sea. This curiosity did not develop into scientific research until later still.

The hallmark for this adventure was greed—gold fever. The compass pointed away from Europe, down the west side of Africa, across the Atlantic to the Caribbean, up the eastern coast of North America and then back to Europe.

That was the geography lesson.

Now, let's put humans into it

Written history is mostly about men, whether they be rogues or heroes.

In this book I am telling the stories of women: brave and loving women who protected their families through slavery; women who brought us to this time in our history.

Sharing these stories with everyone including senior high school students, will start many discussions from which we will learn, understand and appreciate who we are and the opportunities these women have opened up for us

…Now, read on…

The history of discovery is about to repeat itself. Planet Earth is reaching out to find new planets.

In the meantime, let us consider how we discovered, in the 15th century (1400s) that our Earth planet was larger than we thought. We confirmed it when we sailed across the Atlantic Ocean and discovered the New World.

Comparative Ideas in preparing for exploration: 15th century versus 21st century.

Requirements in the 15th century for navigating the Atlantic Ocean:

- The speculative idea was that India was approachable by crossing the Atlantic Ocean.

- Plan: Approach India by crossing the Atlantic Ocean.

- Requirements for getting to India included:

    o   Larger wooden ships with sails (sails are tensile structures powered by wind).

    o   Large wooden oars, which were needed when the wind abated.

- o   Rope made of hemp, fishing lines, an anchor, long knives for protection from pirating ships, large wooden barrels for collecting rain water, lanterns, a compass to indicate the direction of the North Pole, pickled meats, hard biscuits, dried fruit, strong men to learn how to become fighting sailors and most importantly, a captain under the English flag.

Requirements for space exploration in the 21st century:

- Scientific knowledge—repeated experimentation for improving navigation and specifications for spaceships, tools, visualization of landing docks, etc.

- Nations willing to share space discoveries.

- Swift and reliable communication systems.

- Data-sharing with universities.

- Space station supplies.

- Astronaut training.

…and so on.

Chapter 1

Our route to the Caribbean

A complementary thumb-nail tour through European Trading (15th – 19th centuries)

We will begin our tour in the 15th century. There is some information that you need to know about that time.

Excitement in Europe

The 15th century offered adventure, which promised wealth.

Everyone knew at that time that India had gold, other metals and spices, and indeed there was trade in these products. However, the established routes to India were long, difficult and dangerous, involving travel through many countries.

An easier route that eliminated these obstacles would be more desirable. Perhaps this could be achieved by crossing the *seawater* from port to port. A direct route would lead to an increase in trade, and with it profitability. *It was arguments like these that got explorers planning.*

Queen Isabella of Spain became the patron for Christopher Columbus (1492) for such a trial voyage. Christopher Columbus returned from his voyage west with a variety of treasures. He also brought the news that precious metals were scattered all around. Yes, there were natives who may own these metals, but they seemed unaware of the value.

What Christopher Columbus did not know was that he was not in India but on the east coast of America. He named the first group of islands, he discovered, the 'West Indies', considering them to be on the west coast of India. He called the people living on the mainland of America, "Indians" as he thought he had reached India. In the 1900s, these people came to be known as Amerindians. (Notice the name of India keeps popping up).

The news about the new discovery of Indian wealth across the Atlantic Ocean spread throughout Europe like a tornado. The European countries started building boats to find exactly what Columbus had discovered.

Britain was relatively late in getting the news about Columbus' discovery. When Queen Elizabeth I got the news she sponsored and sent a trusted friend, Walter Raleigh, to the Americas to bring back treasure. In the meantime Britain started to build larger ships.

Spain, Netherlands, France, Germany, Denmark, Norway and Portugal offered maritime sponsorships to sail across the Atlantic. For other sea captains not so fortunate to have sponsors, piracy was an obvious choice. With smaller, faster ships, the pirates could attack the larger vessels when they were most vulnerable.

Walter Raleigh, after trying to set up a colony in Virginia, returned to Britain with a load of tobacco in 1586. Tobacco became an important product for England. The positive results of growing tobacco in the southern lands in the Atlantic proved the land there to be fertile; but the local tribes were not inclined to work in agriculture.

Trade

New workers were needed to work in the tropical fields.

It was considered that the agricultural community of serfs* in England would not be able to cope in unaccustomed hot tropical climates. Labour would have to come from elsewhere. Britain learned from the other European countries that there was free labour available by entrapping Africans to work in the West Indies.

Britain also needed ships. Most of Britain's beautiful forests were cut down to provide timber for shipbuilding. *Heart of Oak Are Our Ships*, a British Navy song written in 1740 illustrates this.

The trunks of Britain's oak trees provided the timber for shipbuilding. The branches of the oak trees were cast into furnaces for smelting iron ore. Another usage of the branches was to create fire to boil *seawater* to crystalize salt for curing meat for the voyages.

To colonize the islands on the south western Atlantic, Britain needed agricultural workers from Africa. The method of obtaining these workers was to barter and not to use currency, but to simply exchange goods for Africans.

The British realized that on the west coast of Africa, the cooking utensils and farming implements were outdated and inefficient. They offered to replace pottery vessels and stone tools with metal pots and metal farming tools in exchange for Africans who were already captives and prisoners as a result of inter-tribal warfare. This was a successful barter, they thought.

However, it was not long before the African chiefs ran short of prisoners. The chiefs now had to wage war on other tribes to find more prisoners. Later on, the English traders advanced the market by offering guns to the tribal chiefs. Now, tribal warfare escalated with the increasing thirst for the practical metal equipment; and so entrapping slaves for economic reasons instead of through war became accepted among some African tribes.

Britain made Ghana her port of entry

Britain established 'holding forts' in Ghana, (ironically called "castles") for the African prisoners. The plan was to populate the West Indies with enslaved* Ghanaians who would be controlled by British planters. The British planters were assured protection by the British Navy, provided the planters paid taxes. This was the beginning of Britain's trade and colonialization of the New World.

In my mind's eye, I can see the first British ships sailing on the *seawater* toward Ghana. The Ghanaians must have been mesmerized by the sight of these strange objects on the horizon, growing larger every minute. The young Ghanaian men, curious to examine more, might have dived into the *seawater* to touch the strange sea creatures. These young men mysteriously never returned. They were not missed immediately, because of the excitement of the village gazing at the sea creatures carrying strange white men.

Then the bargaining began...

*Serfs. 11th Century to 1575.

Britain operated within a feudal system. Britain was divided into counties. In each county there was an Earl or a Lord, who owned it.

The working people living in each county were known as free peasants and not free (serfs).

Serfs did not own land. They were required to work and return to the lord the produce from the land that they were given to farm and in exchange, in lieu of wages, receive a share of meat, potatoes, wheat etc. The serfs had the added responsibility of participating in wars as the lord of the county commanded.

The comparison of Serfdom to Slavery

The difference was that the system of serfdom was traditionally accepted. It had grown out of the British Feudal System and offered limited rights; whereas slavery was the result of capture.

The Africans were entrapped strangers who were taken away from their homes and traditions. These enslaved people had no rights, absolutely.

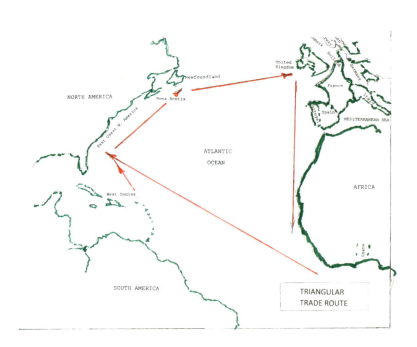

Map – Atlantic Trade Route

Entrapment into slavery in the English Ghanaian castles

This is about a missing brother who became a slave and was imprisoned in the British castle and how 'I', his sister, also became entrapped into slavery.

COME WITH ME

by Doreen Crick
(Entrapment into slavery in Ghana)

"Have you seen my brother?"
    He went that-a-way," she said…
To others,
    I asked.
    "Have you seen my brother?"
They pointed to the distance—
    where large castles stood on the sea shore . . .
As I approached,
    I asked, again…
    "Have you seen my brother?"

I walked down on the sand
    toward the castles on the seashore.
I knocked on the door-—
    "Have you seen my brother?"
"Perhaps," he answered

Come with me.

During the 16th, 17th and 18th centuries, in England and other European countries, young white men were kidnapped from towns situated along the sea coasts. They were taken to boats moored in the harbours to become sailors. Most of these men were considered 'lost at sea'.

COME WITH ME

by Doreen Crick
(Entrapment to becoming a sailor from England.)

"Have you seen my father? I asked
    "He went that-a-way," they said
To another, I asked,
    "Have you seen my father?"
They pointed to the distant large ships—moored
out beyond the sea shore
As I approached the swishing waves on the beach
    I asked, again
    "Have you seen my father?"

I walked further into the waves
    saw a small boat listing, there

    "Have you seen my father?'
"Perhaps," the sailor replied

Come with me.

Another type of capture

At the very beginning of trading in the West, the Spanish entrapped an African tribe known as 'Maroons,' and took them to Jamaica. The Spanish could not control them because they were already a cohesive, organized tribe.

When the British took Jamaica from the Spanish, they too could not control the Maroons.

The British finally decided to comply with the Maroons request to return to Africa. In 1796 the Maroons left Jamaica on a British ship in-transit via Nova Scotia and finally arrived in Africa in 1800.

(But…not all of the Maroons got on the boat from Jamaica at that time.)

Chapter 2

Immigrants to the Leeward Islands

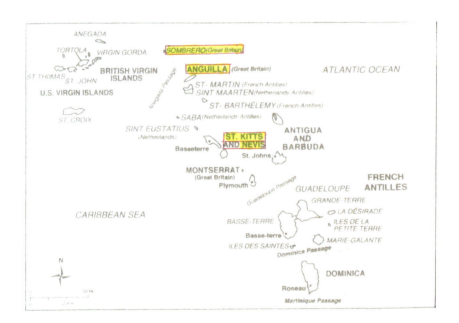

Map – See Anguilla, Nevis, St. Kitts

Settlers from England

The Caribbean islands, 'where the sun shone all year round' were quite an attractive prospect to some. There, on these islands, was an opportunity to find health and wealth.

England at that time was poor (except, of course, for the established gentry). Many common folk were bankrupt and faced debtors' prisons. England needed settlers for her new colonies. She offered to erase the debts of some facing prison, giving them instead the opportunity to become settlers in the Caribbean. The enticing choice was clear: Go west and become a planter in the Caribbean—or go to jail.

England was recovering from the devastation of the black plague. Other infectious diseases were rampant.

- Drinking water became mixed with farm drainage and the result was widespread dysentery.

- Jobs were precariously scarce.

- Many young men were disappearing, and it was rumoured that they were being kidnapped and put onto ships moored in the harbour.

- It was a good time to leave.

The settlers arrived in the Caribbean unprepared for what was needed, but... they knew that Queen Elizabeth I had made a declaration to defend them.

The Enslaved Ghanaians

At first, the enslaved Ghanaians were totally disoriented. Except for the coconut palms on the beach, the environment was strange.

They found themselves tied to poles on a beach in Nevis. *Nevis was a slave market*. Then they were separated into smaller groups.

Non-verbal communication between African women included a slight tilt of the head, lifting eyebrows and expressive movement of the eyes. ("There is a time to speak and there is a time to be silent," as our mothers often warned).

This type of communication instantly came into play between the women from the Ghanaian villages. They were going to keep silent until they understood the plan.

The slavers divided the Ghanaians into four groups. Three groups were divided between Anguilla, St. Christopher and Nevis. From Nevis, the fourth group continued on the boat to other island slave markets and to ports along the East Coast of America.

Britain's Plan for Colonialization

England, after a series of battles with the Caribs, France, Spain and Netherlands, finally colonized these three Leeward Islands, Anguilla, Nevis, and St. Christopher. The Treaty of Versailles in 1782 settled this. St. Christopher, the largest island of the group, was ready for experimentation with growing sugar-cane and cotton.

England had already established a fort at Brimstone Hill in St. Christopher. This fort offered a panoramic view of other Caribbean Leeward Islands and promised protection against any attacks from the sea.

Adaptation and Survival

The Ghanaian women decided to build a village in this difficult situation. They immediately went into high gear and made every effort to protect the children and themselves.

They would follow the rules laid down by the Planter.

The Planter's Rules

1. Enslaved Ghanaians must only speak English or make gestures that they understood. (They obediently followed this rule only when the planter was present).

2. Communication by talking drum* was forbidden.

3. The enslaved Ghanaians must not build fishing boats. The reason for this was to dissuade them from attempting to sail back to Ghana.

How did the English wives adapt to this new culture?

1. The tropical weather was too hot and uncomfortable. They preferred a more temperate climate. They complained that there was nothing exciting to do.

2. They wished their husbands had not persuaded them that everything would be great. There was no gold to be found. They realized that 'finding gold' was a wrong assertion made by their husbands.

3. They yearned to be home again in England with their families and friends.

4. They preferred English food.

5. Many wives returned to England with their children.

The Talking Drum

    The Talking Drum is a traditional instrument. It has two drumheads connected by leather tension cords, around the circumference. The pitch is modulated by squeezing the cords between the body and the arm. By squeezing the top and plucking the strings, different sounds can be made. This drum is used in story-telling and village music.

Chapter 3

Introductions to the three islands – Anguilla, Nevis and St. Christopher (later referred to as St. Kitts)

Anguilla: the smallest of the three islands.

Sandy Ground, Anguilla – where the Salt Pond was formed.

Memories of Anguilla:

My mother's family were Anguillans. Anguillans were great story tellers. Some tales were about living in Anguilla during those early years in slavery. I remember well the aroma of the unleavened bread being baked in the large communal stone oven while we children were listening to stories.

Community oven: Housewives took turns making bread for sharing within the community.

I loved sailing from St. Kitts to visit my family in Anguilla. It was a time for more story-telling. As if relating by script, my mother's people told about events in an orderly fashion, extending almost to the beginning of the 18th century.

I remember sitting on the front steps of my grandparent's home, talking with a woman named Ceita (pronounced 'see-tah'). Ceita told me about her family. She had a head scarf folded and rolled into a doughnut and placed upon her head. This was used to cushion loads that she carried on her head. She removed the scarf and unfolded it. As she did this, she extracted pieces of material from the roll.

"This," she said, "is a piece of a dress my grandmother wore when she was alive." She continued taking out more pieces. Each piece was a treasured memory of a family member who had died.

This head scarf was her family album.

The story of Anguilla

As far as paying taxes to England, Anguilla was a disappointing venture. The soil proved that it was not viable for sugar or cotton production.

The English and Ghanaians in Anguilla were starving. There was a famine. The people became restless. The English landowners and the enslaved Ghanaians met to talk about the scarcity of food.

Considerations:

"We are hungry!"

"If we fight against each other, no-one will win."

The English settlers realized that Anguilla was too small an island to justify a British rescue mission in case of a minor insurrection. Besides, Anguilla was impoverished and had not contributed money to the coffers of Britain.

Previously, the English Anguillans owned all of the land. Now they decided to share the land and to consider the Ghanaians as neighbours. Together, they would work alongside each other for longer hours. The reward was that the Ghanaians would be given the opportunity to eventually own land, if the plan worked.

The plan worked and a bi-cultural community developed, with Ghanaian lands forming a mosaic with English lands. A culture of neighbourliness evolved. This was a success.

The people of Anguilla soon found that pigeon peas, tamarinds, Indian corn and pomegranates grew well. These, they kept for home consumption. They proudly called themselves 'Anguillans.' They built fishing boats and were delighted to catch tropical fish such as grouper, butter fish, snapper, lobster, jack, crab and many other species.

Picking Salt – Anguilla (about 1950)

Later, the Anguillans constructed a salt pond in Sandy Ground. They channelled *seawater* into an artificial pond, where the water evaporated and salt crystals were formed. This was successful. They expanded their operation by building larger vessels to deliver the salt to some of the islands in the Caribbean and for shipment up to Newfoundland.

In Newfoundland, the salt was needed for curing codfish. The skeletal part of the salted cod was then exported down to the sugar plantations for the slaves' diet. It is ironic that around St. Kitts and Nevis, there were delicious species of fish and lobster but the plantation settlers had no access to it without boats. 'No boats', was the rule made by the planters on the sugar and cotton island plantations!

The trade in salt made the Anguillans independent and they were able to build comfortable homes.

Piling Salt – Anguilla.

The Salt Ponds closed in 1985.

Chapter 4

The Island of Nevis

Nevis with its constant cloud overhead

The island of Nevis is a dormant remnant of a prehistoric stratovolcano. It is part of the strata including the islands of St. Kitts and St. Eustatius. At that time, the *seawater* table was very much lower than it is today.

Seven volcanic centres make up Nevis. The island boasts of healthy natural hot sulphur springs. It has a conical-shaped, high mountain which is generally covered by a white cloud. The early adventurers thought it was snow. Columbus sighted Nevis in 1493 and named it for its appearance— Nevis is derived from the Spanish Nuestra Señora de las Nieves (which means Our Lady of the Snows). Caribs already lived there.

Nevis was the British prime slave market. Nevis was settled in 1628 when Anthony Hilton, an English merchant, moved there from St. Kitts following a murder plot against him. He brought 80 settlers with him and 100 more settlers arrived from England.

Nevis grew in importance to Britain. Between 1675 and 1730, it became the headquarters for the slave market trade for the Leeward Islands, with approximately 6,000 to 7,000 enslaved Africans passing through on route to other islands each year.

The Royal African Ships (English slave ships) sailed directly to Nevis.

Facts about Nevis

- A 1678 census shows a community of Irish people forming 22 percent of the population, existing as either indentured servants or freemen.

- During the 17th century, Nevis outranked large islands like Jamaica in sugar production.

- It was reported in London that the head tax on slaves in Nevis was 384,000 pounds sterling compared to that for St. Kitts and Antigua at 67,000 pounds sterling.

- 20 percent of the British Empire's total sugar production in 1700 was derived from Nevisian plantations.

At the time of the American Revolution, exports from the Caribbean colonies, including Nevis, were worth more than all the exports from the mainland 13 colonies of North America combined.

Enslaved families formed the large labour force on the sugar plantations.

In 1706, the French invaded Nevis in an effort to drive out the English. The English planters burned their fields rather than let the French have them and then they hid in the mountains. It was the enslaved people who took up arms to fight against the French, to protect their families. The slaves' bravery shamed the planters, who were ready to surrender.

After the French invasion, sugar production collapsed on Nevis. The French lost the battle but took the 3,400 slaves they had captured in Nevis to Martinique and sold them to the planters, there. Following the invasion, many Europeans left Nevis. The large plantations shrunk into small lots and the population (both black and white) started small agricultural holdings.

The slave owners were paid a compensation for their loss of property (the slaves) by the Crown.

Chapter 5

The Island of St. Christopher – "St. Kitts"

The entry plaza. (The Circus) Basseterre.

St. Kitts is the modern name for the island of St. Christopher. It is 68 square miles in size. St. Kitts had an unstable start in history. It was one of the first Caribbean islands to be colonized by England. The first settlers had been Caribs followed by the English who shared it with the French. It was finally ceded to Britain by the Treaty of Versailles in 1782.

St. Kitts was developed as a sugarcane and cotton plantation island. The line between 'white settlers' and 'black Ghanaians' was religiously and clearly marked. Rules that slaves should be subservient were understood. The Catholic Church and the Anglican Church were clearly unwelcoming to slaves.

The Ghanaian men slaved in the cotton fields or on the sugar plantations. The Ghanaian men also did the heavy lifting in the construction of the Brimstone Hill Fort, which provided an excellent view of the undulating land stretching down to the *seawater* and beyond, to include the islands of Nevis, Antigua, Saba and St. Eustatius.

Brimstone Hill Fort

During the construction of the Brimstone Hill Fort, the Ghanaian men worked many miles away from the village. They did not return home each day. They lived in little huts made of sugar cane trash. There were no toilets provided.

Sometimes a planter, on the basis of a rumour or suspicion of a revolt, would choose a popular slave for a public whipping. The slave would be whipped mercilessly with a cat o' nine tails.

Introduction to Ethics and Slavery
(a United Nations Document)

Slavery can usually be described as the ownership, buying and selling of human beings for the purpose of forced and unpaid labour.

Article 1, Universal Declaration of Human Rights

Everyone has the right to life, liberty and security of person.

Article 3, Universal Declaration of Human Rights

No one shall be held in slavery or servitude; slavery and the slave trade in all their forms shall be prohibited

Women from Ghana made the villages safe for the children.

The Ghanaian women immediately got in tune with the new environment. They were to work in the fields, or as domestic servants in the homes of the planters. They cooperated with the rules that the Europeans made: The rules were:

- Speak in English to the Europeans.
- No talking drums.
- No fishing boats.
- Do not make eye-contact with the Europeans.
- Be quick and clean in your duties.
- Never say 'no' to a European.

Everything was so unfamiliar at first, until the Ghanaian women noticed coconut palms on the island. They knew that coconut water was healthy to drink. They took the fibre of the coconut and made mats and mattresses. They used the coconut oil for cooking and the grated nut for making cakes and breads.

Doreen Crick

You had none of these:

"A poem to you, Auntie".

Looking from our 21st Century to yours into the 17th Century —

 I cringe in my understanding about your Orientation, Auntie,

 *Your **Time** is frightening to me!*

Quick rules of one's Orientation are as a psychologist would indicate;

 *A realistic awareness of **Place**, **Time** and **Person**.*

 You were gifted with none of these as a colonised slave!

Your Orientation to **Place**:

 Place: Ghana? A Colonial island? Did anyone tell you where you were?

Your Orientation to **Time**:

 What did "yesterday" mean to you? "How did you count **Time** without a calendar?"

*Your Orientation to **Person**:*

Who was your mother? You were probably taken as a child from one plantation to another. Today, we still have the tradition of calling older women "Auntie" for she might be a relative.

I love the three tools you sensibly used for the survival of yourself and your family:

Communication with your eyes to your family, as a warning.

By acting the part of being "happy".

"Yes, boss, I sing 'cos I am happy!"

"Yes, boss, you is a good man!"

By using the triple negative:

"No, boss, I ain't seen nothin'."

And most importantly, for being "Auntie" to the child given to you from another plantation.

We the children of the 21st. Century, do honour you…

European Wives.

The English wives were mostly frustrated with the situation. They missed home and social interaction with family and friends. They missed the freedom of being in an English village and eating English food. And strangely, they missed the English weather and fog.

They were homesick. Their husbands were now very different. They were no longer partners in a marriage bed, for they had extended their sexual behaviors with a new arrogance. They had smashed the protective, sacred shell of marriage and had become crude. Talking with the Parish Priest offered no comfort.

They had tried to be friendly with the 'slave domestics' at first, but now found themselves habitually watching for enticing signals from their husbands to the enslaved housemaids.

They realized that they had become suspicious of everyone. They developed the art of tiptoeing quietly to listen in on conversations. They watched for babies of mixed parentage. Many wives left St. Kitts and Nevis with their children and returned to England. They had no wish to return to the Caribbean. The planters were lonely and sad, at first. They realized that their families would never return.

The relationships with their children on the plantation became closer. They sent these children to Barbados or to England for further education. They deeded their estates to them. This was the beginning of a new social structure in the Caribbean—the mixed shade dimension of the new middle class of the future.

In the Ghanaian enslaved families, there were many babies. There are no statistics for the number of survivals. However, the effect of poor housing and being strapped on the backs of mothers while working in the cotton fields in the hot sun, must have taken a toll on their survival

Singing in the cotton fields helped to quiet the babies. Singing in the cotton fields also communicated where each Ghanaian was situated in the field. A missing singing voice indicated an alert!

At an early age the children were made to work in the cotton fields though sometimes an older woman who could not pick cotton or cut sugar cane was permitted to stay at home in charge of the babies.

Village community gathering and storytelling

Village Storytelling

In Ghana, it was the village custom to share story telling at night when the moon was bright, or the sky showing a dome of stars. Village news was exchanged. Unbelievable, humorous stories about escaping wild animals were told.

These stories often triggered laughter. Teenagers jovially challenged each other. It was all in fun.

Back in Ghana, the village felt safe and strong. The village was the community where everyone knew each other's Ghanaian name and became responsible for helping to raise each child. Upon being enslaved, the women's decision was to keep the community as strong as it was before the slavers took them from Ghana and so the Ghanaians continued the tradition of open-air village meetings. This was their opportunity to speak the village language.

Sometimes, one particular elder would tell the Anansi story as the group sat around. The elders developed a code for sharing information or a warning. This code was included within the Anansi story. The domestic maids would listen in on the conversations in the planters' houses. The information they heard might be good or bad. The news might be about searching for a particular slave, or it might be about transactions being planned for the estate. The elders would insert the information into the Anansi story. The genius was in changing the story just a little so as not to make the children become aware of the change.

This method of 'information sharing' allowed the children to tell the Anansi stories openly in English, even in the presence of the planter. The planter was unaware of the significance of the story to the slaves and the children were unaware of the slight deviation within the story.

This code was absolutely necessary for the safety of the village. Anansi stories have survived even today.

The character of Anansi was that of a selfish lout (actually, Anansi was a spider). Anansi considered himself to be the 'centre of the world' and always had to be winning. The Ghanaians gave the character role of "Anansi" to the planter (without ever letting it be known).

There are many folktales told about Anansi.

Let's share the story: ANANSI AND THE BANANAS

Once upon a time, all the animals worked in the fields daily, but Anansi, the spider, sat on his porch enjoying the sun.

One of the industrious animals noticed that Anansi had not planted a vegetable garden and that his wife and three children were becoming thin from starvation. The neighbour offered Anansi four bananas with the instructions that there was only one banana for each child and one banana for the wife. The neighbour apologized but, he said, he had not brought a banana for Anansi.

For breakfast on the following morning, Anansi set the table with five plates but there was nothing on his plate. There he sat with an empty plate, looking very sad.

The Ghanaian children listening to the story saw the irony of this and would laugh about Anansi's dilemma.

"Oh… oh papa," said one of Anansi's children, "please have half of my banana."

"Oh, no." said Anansi, "The kind gentleman said that I could not have any."

The Ghanaian children again saw the irony of this and would again laugh.

"Oh, papa, you must have it. I cannot watch you starve to death!" And so Anansi reluctantly accepted half of his daughter's banana.

It was not long before the second, the third child and even his wife insisted that Anansi should have half of their bananas as well.

Ultimately, Anansi had two bananas for breakfast and the females in his family made themselves content with their scrappy halves.

This story was often repeated in length with lots of drama: Each child would speak in an entreating voice, "P-l-e-a-s-e Papa!" and finally the dear wife, with tears in her eyes, would beg him to have her half of her banana so that he would not die.

Generally, there was laughter around telling the Anansi stories in the village. Everyone knew that life was unfair and hopeless on the plantation.

The little bits of news the women would tuck into the Anansi dialogue helped to keep the community safe and the children openly told the story about Anansi and they did not include the code.

Food on the plantation.

Cattle, sheep, goats and chickens survived the passage across the Atlantic. Pigs were brought from Africa and some wild fowl. These were carefully farmed. Turkeys were introduced from America. Meats had to be pickled with salt. (*Seawater* in shallow basins open to the sun would crystalize into salt.). When a cow was too old to produce milk, it was slaughtered. The choice pieces of beef were pickled or cooked immediately in celebration with other European planters. Meat and fish were scarce for the slaves. Only scraps were given to them.

The other parts of the animal, the hoof, tail and head, were given to the slaves. These have become special Caribbean dishes such as ox-tail soup, souse and black pudding. For a fish dish, 'Salt-fish and ackee' (egg) was created out of the skeletal portion of the salted cod, but served with the bones removed.

Chapter 6

The Promise of Freedom

The housemaids were the first to hear it… "slavery is wrong" was the news arriving from England.

There was a "buzz" in the planter's house. This "buzz" vibrated into the Anansi stories.

Meanwhile, at the beginning of the 19th century, the English parliament made a law that everyone living in England was free. Several planters, who had brought their slaves with them to England from the colonies, were disappointed now, because their slaves refused to return to the colonies with them.

A freedom movement started in England. The movement spread outside the established churches (the Catholic Church and the Church of England), to newer churches: the Methodist and Scottish Churches. The freedom movement inspired English housewives to begin knocking on neighbors' doors to stop them from purchasing tobacco and rum arriving from America, where slavery was rampant.

'Freedom' was declared, by the new churches, 'the Right of every Human'. The new Methodist Church sent evangelical preachers to the Americas, to extend the new mission to enslaved peoples and to teach them about Jesus.

Christianity Extended

The Methodist missionaries received no cooperation from the planters in St. Kitts. The planters asserted that one hour on Sunday for slaves to hear about Jesus would be too costly for their plantations to consider. The house slaves heard the heated arguments between the planters and the Methodists. The house slaves decided - what the missionaries were offering must be good!

The Methodist preacher told the Ghanaian women that he wanted to help them by saving their souls and they were happy to let him. In 1760 the slaves met with the Methodist preacher before sunrise in a specified field as planned. There, they learned about Christianity.

One of the things that the slaves also wanted to learn was to read; especially, to be able to read those documents that "massa"(the planter) had on his desk.

"Will you teach us to read?" the women asked the preacher and the preacher agreed to teach them. Secret Christian worship and church schools began in the fields before sunrise. Later, the discovery that many slaves were able to read was a surprise to the planters.

Acceptance of a new Faith.

Before arriving in the Leeward Islands, the Ghanaians worshiped the great God Nyame, the Supreme Creator who controlled the sun, the moon, the stars and the crops.

The story about Jesus, 'the only Son of God', was at first puzzling. The Ghanaians questioned, "How could this great creator allow his only son to suffer and be killed?" This was very puzzling.

"Well," they reasoned, "Let's perhaps consider Jesus as a friend, for He, too, suffered."

They began to hum and to sing about Jesus while they picked cotton in the fields. They began to consider him as a trusted friend, perhaps as a brother and even a comforter. Hundreds of Negro Spirituals have survived the cotton fields of slavery. Sometimes, we find ourselves humming a happy cheery tune; or perhaps, in times of sorrow, a cry for divine support. Then we realize that the Spiritual we were singing, was a 'scrap' from the cotton fields.

Freedom from slavery was declared by Great Britain on Monday, August 1, 1834 but the Caribbean Islands were not ready; the slaves had to work for an additional four years without payment. Their occupation was renamed 'apprenticeship'. As an old enslaved person might have said, "the old, retired leaky slave ship still refuses to sink!"

"De-meaning"—A rant

By Doreen Crick

The enslaved person asked, "What is *de-meaning* of 'Slavery over'?" *'De-meaning'* ironically grew into a *'demeaning attitude', a survival demeanour.*

What is *de- meaning* of' Slavery over' for us black people? Does it mean we are going home, to our villages in Africa?

The boss gave us *'de meaning'*. He said, "It means that you are still free to work for me. Nothing has changed. Freedom is just an English word. You cannot swim back to Africa."

"Should we be joyful?"

What is *'de-meaning'* written on those Freedom papers?

If we even saw the Freedom papers, we are unable to read *'de-meaning'* on them!

Our questions about *'de-meaning'* of the Freedom papers are—free to do what? Is this a freedom trick?

"Where can we live?"

"Slavery is over!" "What is *'de-meaning'* of "slavery over?

"*De meaning* was 'nowhere else to go except to remain a slave on the plantation.' "Leave empty-handed," the boss said.

What is *de-meaning* of 'freedom'?

Before, it meant we survived as animals. We never owned shelter, farm tools, buckets, free access to water and seeds to grow.

Now—What is "*de-meaning*" of Freedom and Emancipation?"

The immediate result of Emancipation was that—

The planters remained in control. They expected freed slaves to remain subservient and (guess what?) Demeaned. Europeans prided themselves on preventing Africans access to independence and wealth.

Ironically, England compensated the planters with money for the loss of slaves! On paper, slavery was renamed 'apprenticeship' for four more years.

Afterwards, freed slaves built shacks on sticks on the flood plains and continued to work on the plantations from sun-up to sun-down.

The option to be free could not be exercised for many years for economic reasons.

Chapter 7

The experience of slaves along the Eastern Seaboard of North America

These are the reflections of newly enslaved Africans:

"We were living in our home village community in Africa. The slavers brought us to America, where our community life was fractured. We were sold, each of us to a different planter."

The American planters' plan

The planters bought each of their slaves from a different slave boat; one slave from an English slave boat, one slave from a French slave boat, one slave from a Spanish slave boat, one slave from the Dutch slave boat, one slave from the Norwegian slave boat and perhaps one slave from a pirate slave boat.

This mixed gang of slaves was bought and taken to a plantation to work. These slaves were strangers to each other. No family. No stories to share. No memories or jokes to share about Mother Africa.

"Who are you?" I wanted to ask the African shackled to me; but his eyes seemed to be asking the same questions.

"Where am I? Where is my family?" These questions are storming in my head. So, we do not know each other.

This is the planter's trick to keep us apart.

> *"A man without ebony in his skin carries a bull-whip in his hand. He lashes the air—once, twice. Each time it makes a whirring sound. He points his finger at each of us and raises his fist. He waves the whip in the direction he wishes us to follow. Our feet follow. Confusion explodes in my head. The hot sun is cold and my feet are . . . freezing."*

Our Christian confirmation of faith:

The hymns that the English people sing are about the sea: a lighthouse, light on the shore, God's arm strong to save, restless waves…

The spirituals that the enslaved people sang were about searching for freedom and running away. The words in the Spirituals told us where to go, for example, down by the river, the North Star, a chariot.

Still today, after a church Service, we do not ask if the minister preached a good sermon; instead we ask, 'What is the message?'

The Negro Spirituals used their words as messages to the congregation to share an escape route at the planning stage (of course, since no slaves came back, it was never known if the route was secure for travelling).

Imagine walking north along the Mississippi and up to Canada! During the War of Independence, the slaves referred to Canada as 'the promised land'; very few made it to Canada.

Why was Canada recognized as the 'promised land'? The English king had promised safety in Canada to the Loyalists and slaves who would fight for him during the American War of Independence (1775–1783). Canada, especially Nova Scotia, was offered as a sanctuary.

Many Quakers and other Christian white folk helped slaves who were heading north by hiding them in wagons piled high with hay and providing safe houses along the route. They gave them food and shelter. These white people were in danger for harbouring escaped slaves. They, too had codes of communication for assisting run-away slaves.

England promised freedom

England had promised freedom three times before. Finally, it took effect (somewhat, at least) on the fourth promise, the *Proclamation of 1834*.

The first promise was made to the Loyalists arriving in Canada from America in the 1775 War of Independence.

The second promise was to the Jamaica Maroons (1796). They sailed from Canada to Sierra Leone in 1800 as promised by the British.

The third promise was to the black soldiers from Quebec/Ontario following the last part of the American War of Independence, 1812.

The fourth proclamation was in 1834. This affected the whole of the Western British Empire, but not the Caribbean Islands, for another four years.

…and the world was not ready.

The QUESTION for your discussion and debate is: Since exploration into the west was not perfect or completed… are we ready for another adventure, for a new discovery, for man to move to space?

Still Standing

by Doreen Crick

We know for sure – that it started in the 15th century.

And now we are **here...**

        And still standing.

They came for us—and piled us

Into the bellies of their sailing boats

Auctioned us off at their devilish markets. (despite that)

        We are still standing.

Made us hungry, so that we begged for bread

Kidnapped our freedom, just to make themselves 'feel good'

(Despite that) **We are still standing.**

We knew better...

        We knew that was not the Creator's plan

We knew there was a Time for correction

        And so... We are still standing.

Did the Bible say... Sin was black?

Did the Bible say... Good and God were white?

Who cultivated these terrible assumptions?

Was this a conspiracy made on the top decks of those ships?

Perhaps so... But with God's help

        We are still standing

Chapter 8

READ ALL ABOUT IT: BLACKSTRAP MOLASSES…

Information alert!

Shhh… shhh… a secret! A St. Kitts discovery in the mid-20th century! The St. Kitts planters had shared this information with the slaves: "Blackstrap molasses will make you sick and will cause diarrhoea. It is only good for animals".

Three hundred years later, a World Health Organization representative found that the children in St. Kitts were anaemic—lacking in iron.

"Why," she asked, "should this happen when there is so much blackstrap molasses being produced on the island?"

The nutritional profile of blackstrap molasses shows it as a significant source of Iron, Copper, Magnesium, Potassium, Vitamin B6, Selenium and a good source of Calcium. It has a lower sugar content than refined molasses or crystalized sugar.

For almost two hundred years, the planters in St. Kitts gave away blackstrap molasses because, 'it has no value,' the planters said. In the meantime, blackstrap molasses was being eaten on toast or porridge by Colonists along the Eastern coast of North America, across the Atlantic to England and Europe.

It was later discovered that blackstrap molasses was being used as the main ingredient for the distillation of rum. Rum became very popular for sailors and everyone. A lucrative rum trade was started in the colonies. England wanted to benefit from the rum trade through taxes. Rum-runners refused to pay the taxes. Enforcement became difficult as the Rum-runners built faster and faster fake 'fishing boats'.

The question still remains: Who got the money from the molasses?

St. Kitts later built a modern 20th century sugar factory but the demand for sugar started to decline toward the end of the 20th century as beet sugar from America and Europe started replacing cane sugar in St. Kitts.

Today St. Kitts now needs to catch up with the demands of the 21st century; but St. Kitts has no 'investments' or money for financing a new industry.

The sugar factory was shut down and abandoned. King Sugar is dead.

Voices from the shores of the Caribbean

The Seawater has erased our footprints from the sands, but we were here. No historians have written about us. The corrupt sugar and cotton plantations have shrunk into the pockets of the planters.

NOW, we say

"Let us *freely* play a village game for
 "The field is ours
  And the ball is ours."

New Rules of engagement:

"Each team will pick players of unequal strengths and talents
 We will support each player's unique talent.

The goal post is **knowledge.**
 Of the past,
  and for engaging our future."

And that is what

our Women from the shores of the

Caribbean Leeward Islands said.

Readings of interest.

Blackman, Francis W., *John Wesley 300*, 2003

Ching, Rev. Donald S., *Forever Beginning*, 1960

Grant, John N., *Maroons in Nova Scotia*, 2002

Innis, Sir. Probyn, *Historic Basseterre*, 1979

Jensen, Albert C., *Cod* (1944)

Life in the 17th Century, http://academics.triton.edu/uc/rotnfaml.htm

Sherwood, Marika, *Britain, Slavery—Trade in enslaved Africans*, 2007

Multiple Authors, *Guiana Methodist District "Kindling of the Flames"*

Rogozinski, Jan, *Brief history of the Caribbean*, 1994

St. Johnston, Sir Reginald, *French Invasion of St. Kitts-Nevis*, 1936

Shepard & Beckles, *Caribbean Slavery*, 2000

The Guardian UK Paper, *Slavery-Abolition-Compensation*, 2018

Walker, James W. St. G., *Black Loyalists (1783 – 1870)*, 1976

Wikipedia (2-25-2017) *Atlantic Slave Trade*

Wikipedia (4-7-2017) *Navigation Act*

Wikipedia (9-22-2016) *Triangular Trade*

World Culture Encyclopedia, *Culture of Ghana* (history, people, clothing, Traditions, women, beliefs, food customs http://www.everyculture.com/Ge-it/Ghana.html

Ethics and Slavery: http://www.bbc.co.uk/ethics/slavery/ethics/intro_1.shtml